Cryptocurrency

Best Strategies for Investing and

Profiting from Cryptocurrency

Mark Clarkson

Table of Contents

Introduction

Congratulations on purchasing *Cryptocurrency: Best Strategies for Investing and Profiting from Cryptocurrency* and thank you for doing so.

If you are like many others around the world, the highs that Bitcoin rose to during the holiday season of 2017 have convinced you that now is the time to learn more about this whole cryptocurrency craze. Luckily, there are plenty of other options out there that are experiencing similar levels of growth, while at the same time not costing $14,000 or more per unit.

To help you get started investing successfully, the following chapters will discuss everything you need to know about cryptocurrency and how to get started investing. First, you will learn all about the ins and outs of the principles of cryptocurrency and what you need to know to start investing effectively. Next, you will learn all about some of the most interesting cryptocurrencies on the market today. From there, you will learn all about investing in cryptocurrency in the long-term, and the special considerations this requires. Finally, you will learn about investing in cryptocurrency in the short-term, along with strategies to help you do so effectively.

There are plenty of books on this subject on the market, thanks again for choosing this one! Every effort was made to ensure it is full of as much useful information as possible, please enjoy!

Chapter 1: A Primer on Cryptocurrency

In the holiday season by the end of 2017, Bitcoin created headlines all around the world. It has been talked in the media because of its rollercoaster price. You may have heard about the fuzz but do not know what exactly is happening. There are a lot to learn about digital currencies. There are different ins and outs that you need to learn to understand fully the heart of the matter. Not to mention, the jargon that comes with cryptocurrencies. Fret not! You are not alone. In fact, only about 50% of the population can accurately articulate the broad points of cryptocurrency and blockchain technology, and only about 10% interact with them in with any degree of regularity. That means, there are still a lot of people who are yet to understand the whatnots of cryptocurrency

Here's the short version of explanation. You can think of cryptocurrency the way you would with PayPal, except that the cryptocurrency you are working with isn't based on a traditional currency and the transaction is completely anonymous. To explain more completely, the term cryptocurrency applies to any sort of digital currency that is based around cryptographic processes and computer code which generates its price exclusively based on what can be justified via supply and demand. Cryptocurrencies would not be possible without blockchain technology (discussed below). Because there is currently far more interest in investing in cryptocurrency than there is in using it for traditional purposes, speculative investors tend to exert a greater than average level of control over the price movement which is enough to leave the entire market extremely volatile.

As Bitcoin represented the original proof of concept for the technology, it has remained at the top of the pile, and as of January 2018 it is worth about $14,500, making it the most expensive cryptocurrency on the market today with a market capitalization rate of more than $30 billion, more than half the total for cryptocurrency overall. Bitcoin's main competition is the Ethereum Platform, which is currently making strides among both businesses and consumers thanks to its overall commitment to blockchain technology as a whole, as well as smart contracts, which are simple programs that can be triggered when certain external events occur.

These are only the big two, of course, the market is currently diverse enough to support more than a thousand different types of cryptocurrency. While some of these are simply minor Bitcoin clones that are looking to cash in on the next big thing, others contain their own unique strengths that allow them to stand on their own two feet and offer the perfect service to a certain subset of people.

While traditional, also known as fiat, currencies are always going to be limited in their movement due to their explicit ties to the economy of a given country, cryptocurrencies routinely see movement based on events that occur around the world. Anything can affect the price of a given cryptocurrency as long as enough of its investors believe that the issue is relevant. For this reason, and others, cryptocurrencies run the gamut from being worth less than $0.01 all the way up to Bitcoin's maximum value of $20,000 per unit.

As a general rule, cryptocurrencies come in two varieties, centralized and decentralized. All of the cryptocurrencies on the market today are decentralized, which means that they operate in a completely autonomous fashion, devoid of any type of guiding authority pulling the strings. In contrast to these, you can find centralized cryptocurrencies such as the cryptocurrency China is currently hard at work on or the

CryptoRubble that Russia announced it was working on near the end of 2017. Those that are decentralized are almost always going to require additional levels of verification to guarantee that any transactions which go through are completely accurate and aren't used for malicious purposes.

Blockchain details

Blockchain is the technology that makes cryptocurrency possible. A blockchain is a decentralized database with nodes that can be placed literally anywhere in the world. While the technology has only been around for about a decade, it is already under consideration for adoption at virtually every level of society – from financial services to healthcare. It has earned this reputation for security and accessibility; thanks to its ability to provide read-only access to important information to anyone who needs it while at the same time ensuring that the data itself remains extremely secure.

Each block in the blockchain contains a wide variety of different transactions, along with information that allows the blockchain to automatically sort its blocks correctly. This is a complicated process that starts with two individuals completing a cryptocurrency transaction. Every time enough transactions are collected by a node, they are uploaded into a block, and this block of transactions is then verified by a third party, colloquially known as a cryptocurrency miner, who is using a high-powered computer to verify that the block is legitimate before passing it along to the blockchain.

This block is then held up to a secondary round of scrutiny and is then added to the blockchain if, and only if, 51 percent of all the currently active nodes agree with the information that it contains. If this is the case, then the information is added to the blockchain, and the data stored in each node is then updated to reflect the new blockchain. This happens each time a new block is added to a blockchain, thousands of times per day.

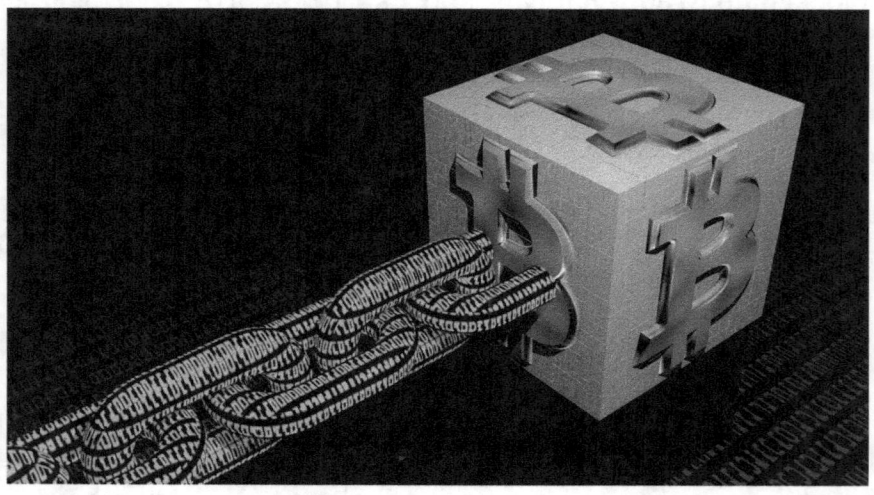

These aspects of blockchain technology make it extremely useful for the types of functions that require it to be self-sorting while at the same time allowing for the blockchain to operate smoothly free of all external control. Rather, the blockchain sorts and verifies its own data while the nodes interact with one another to make it possible for any number of users to interact with the blockchain without worry that things aren't going to be able to sort themselves out.

Users who are interested can look but not touch when it comes to the all of the details of their personal transactions, while other transactions will only display amounts with no information at all given out to make it possible to tie a given transaction to a specific individual. Those who run a node for the blockchain in question are then able to add new blocks to the blockchain, but only if a majority of the blocks on the chain agree that the new information makes sense.

While the nature of blockchain technology makes it extremely secure, this is only because technology as a whole, hasn't reached the point where it needs to be to make this type of hack possible. To create a false block, a scenario would need to be created where enough false nodes were running to indicate that the accurate version of the blockchain was actually inaccurate. While the cost for such an endeavor currently far outweighs the reward, it is unlikely that this will remain that way forever.

Besides the 51 percent rule, every blockchain also has an additional system in place to make sure that no block can be changed after it has already been added to the chain. This is because when a new block is added to the blockchain, it is encoded using something known as a hash function. This means several things, starting with the fact that it would be impossible for anyone to view the full blockchain, even if they managed to get a hold of it, without having the right method of decryption, which is only available to the creator of the blockchain.

The most commonly used hash function is the SHA256 hash, and it also serves to make it easier for the blockchain to sort blocks properly and also acts as a digital fingerprint for the data it holds, if the data changes, so does the hash. After a block is added to the chain and given its own hash, that hash is then factored into the hash of the blockchain as a whole, which is then updated to reflect the change. This hash can then be verified by a program known as a Merkle tree, allowing it to quickly match the hash on file to the current hash and easily spot any illicit changes that may have been made in the interim. Altered data is then purged from the system and replaced with a previously verified copy. Essentially, what this means is that once data is on the blockchain, it will be there for good.

Pricing

When it comes to tracking the prices of various cryptocurrencies, it is important to keep in mind that while they are not controlled in the traditional sense, they still follow the rules of supply and demand. In fact, without all the interference that more traditional currencies experience, many experts believe they represent these ideas more fully than their compatriots. Just because no one is pulling the strings doesn't mean that the price of cryptocurrency isn't tied to external events, however. In fact, they are often more closely tied to events all around the world as there is no telling what could set them off.

Furthermore, when it comes to pricing in general, cryptocurrencies will be far more likely to be affected by the type of speculative manipulation than other types of assets typically are. This is caused by the fact that there are far more people investing for speculative purposes than there are for practical purposes. This, in turn, creates a pricing bubble that takes the current price outside the bounds of what supply and demand dictate. This problem is heavily magnified in smaller cryptocurrencies as there could only be a few thousand people with units anywhere, so every new acquisition carries potential weight.

The basics of cryptocurrency trading take place in much the same way that any other sort of trading does. Those looking to purchase cryptocurrencies try to buy low from those who already own the cryptocurrency who are interested in selling their units at the greatest rate the market will stand. As cryptocurrency, especially the smaller variations, are known to see as much as 15 percent movement in price each day, the amount that can be gained or lost in a single day can be immense if caution isn't taken during the undertaking.

Due to the extremely speculator focused nature of the cryptocurrency market in 2018, it is extremely difficult to not find a cryptocurrency listed on the major exchanges that aren't experiencing some degree of pricing bubble. This is not necessarily a bad thing, however, as long as the price you buy in at is close enough to the market value price that you won't be caught with your pants down should the bubble pop and the price return to normal. If you do buy in too late, then you risk losing out as the price will quickly drop past what you paid with a clear indication it won't be turning around again anytime soon.

Price can also be influenced by a wide variety of external factors, either for the positive or the negative. One of the most common ways this affects most cryptocurrency is through the use of automated trading bots to boost liquidity. Liquidity is crucial for a cryptocurrency to flourish, but it requires a delicate balance as a liquidity level that is too high indicates that no one is interested in buying into the cryptocurrency, while a liquidity level that is too low means that no one is able to buy, even if they want to.

Automated trading bots, most frequently deployed from China, solve this problem in multiple ways. First, they trade back and forth with one another, generating liquidity that other traders can see and base their own assumptions on. These trades can also be picked off by actual traders who are looking to complete either one side or the other of the equation. Finally, as the bot transactions still need to be mined as if they were any other blockchain transaction, the bot trading process actually helps to generate addition units of cryptocurrency thanks to the rewards that are generated from mining the block.

While liquidity and other external forces can be used to combat artificial deflation the cryptocurrency might be experiencing, it can also be used for selfish purposes to perpetrate what is known as a pump and dump. Using this strategy, an investor buys up as much of the asset in question as possible before doing everything in their power to push the price to obscene highs that they can then cash in on by selling all of their assets all at once.

This strategy is especially effective with cryptocurrency as no two exchanges are connected which means that all that someone would need to do to execute a pump and dump successfully would be to buy up all the currently available units of a given cryptocurrency in a single exchange before executing the pump and dump as planned.

Chapter 2: Cryptocurrencies to Consider

While Bitcoin's end of 2017 performance made it clear that it is still the king of the hill, that doesn't mean that there aren't plenty of other cryptocurrencies out there that are also worth paying close attention to. This chapter is full of other relevant types of cryptocurrencies that are likely to see serious movement in 2018. It is important to keep in mind that, not only is this going to be just a brief overview, it is also important to keep up to date on your cryptocurrency of choice as things can change extremely quickly which means that the longer it has been since this book was published, the more likely it is that some of the information found here is out of date. The following currencies should be available from any major cryptocurrency exchange.

Ethereum

After Bitcoin, Ethereum is the most popular of all of the cryptocurrency platforms on the market today. Its cryptocurrency, known as ether, is primarily used for the payment of services for applications and smart contracts that run on the Ethereum platform directly. While Bitcoin is focused almost exclusively on person to person transactions, Ethereum is more interested in being a platform for the advancement of blockchain and smart contract technology, with ether serving as an easy way improve interactions. Ether does see a fair amount of speculation as well, however, and one ether is worth about $900 as of January 2018.

Ethereum was created by a Bitcoin programmer by the name of Vitalik Buterin after he wrote a whitepaper in 2013 suggesting a programming language be added to the Bitcoin blockchain. After his suggestion was ignored, Buterin quit his job and spent the next two years getting Ethereum up and running for its July 2015 launch. Ether is used to run the virtual machines that run these applications which rely on gas, or a portion of a single ether, to cover their operating costs to the system as a whole. Roughly 18 million new ether are created every year.

Take note, Ether, in early 2018, will be making a switch from the commonly used proof-of-work validation system to a proof-of-stake validation system. This new system will work by choosing the creator of the next block more or less at random, with each validator (the replacement for miners) being more likely to be chosen the more they have invested in the system. Blocks will then be said to be forged, rather than mined. Forgers will be able to opt-in to the system in exchange for any amount of ether. The amount they choose will then essentially be held hostage, and ownership will be taken away if they do anything shady. Forgers will then receive transaction fees instead of traditional mining rewards.

2017 was a very good year for Ethereum, and while Bitcoin stole the spotlight at the end of the year, it made headlines early on due to the creation of the Ethereum Enterprise Alliance which is a combination of Fortune 500 companies and blockchain companies that are dedicated to increasing the use of blockchain technology worldwide. The organization started with just 30 members, and their numbers topped 100 by the end of 2017. The Alliance is currently working on creating a blockchain that more accurately addresses the interests of the financial and business sectors.

In the blocks of the Ethereum blockchain, smart contracts are stored alongside transaction data and are transferred from node to node just like any other type of data. As such, nodes can sometimes experience longer than normal upload times as the combined drag of all the smart contracts on the chain adds up. Nevertheless, the Ethereum blockchain can process about 25 transactions per second, though that number is expected to increase as the transition to the proof-of-stake system takes place.

Bitcoin cash

One of Bitcoin's biggest problems is that its blockchain is built on first-generation technology. While this is understandable as it was the first of its kind, it has had a problem processing the number of transactions that its popularity has required for quite some time. What's more, despite the community's tireless work on the problem, it doesn't appear to be going away anytime soon. One bottleneck in the issue is the fact that the blocks in the Bitcoin blockchain are limited in size to just a single megabyte. Added to this issue is that the blockchain is only able to process about seven transactions per second, at its peak.

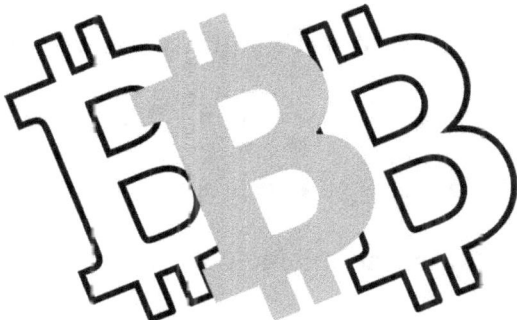

Bitcoin cash is the latest and most direct way to date of handling this issue. It was created by placing a hard fork in the Bitcoin blockchain on August 1, 2017. The biggest difference between it and the traditional Bitcoin blockchain is the fact that its block size limit is eight times that of the standard blockchain. This alone allows it to process eight times as many transactions without having to do any additional work on the blockchain infrastructure.

This hard fork came about in response to the application of the Bitcoin Improvement Proposal that took effect in July 2017. This proposal restructured the way the data in the traditional blockchain blocks was viewed by the blockchain, tricking it into thinking that the data is smaller than it actually is. The part of the community that is now a part of Bitcoin Cash felt that this would only delay the confrontation of the true problem that the cryptocurrency is currently facing, which is the inherent lack of scalability of the platform. Additionally, the BIP serves to strengthen the position of those who wish to treat Bitcoin as a speculative investment as opposed to an actual currency.

As such, Bitcoin Cash has already developed something of a reputation when it comes to being the cryptocurrency for those who actually want to spend their cryptocurrency. It contains all of the transaction data of the original blockchain, up until block 478558 and its first unique block as 478559. At the same time, Bitcoin Cash started using what is known as the Emergency Difficulty Adjustment algorithm for mining purposes which immediately made it nearly twice as profitable to mine as traditional bitcoins, though only on an erratic basis.

This level of fluctuation continued until November 2017 when the algorithm was rewritten to provide additional stability. While it took the market a little while to catch on,

Bitcoin Cash has only grown in popularity since its arrival on the market and is now listed on many of the most popular exchanges including Kracken, Bitstamp, and Coinbase where it can be found as either BCC or BCH on the trading ticker. One Bitcoin Cash was worth approximately $2,500 in December 2017.

Ripple

While Bitcoin was the talk of the town at the end of 2017, it was the only cryptocurrency experiencing growth far beyond anyone's expectations. Ripple (XRT) started off December 2017 trading at just $0.25 cents per unit, and by December 31 it was up to more than $2.50. This 1,000 percent price increase has since made it the second most profitable cryptocurrency by market cap, second only to the unflappable bitcoin.

What's even better for its long-term prospects is the fact that its price increase didn't just come about in response to the movement Bitcoin was experiencing. Rather, it was a perfectly natural response to numerous different positive events that all took place in the same month. First, Ripple completed a lockup of its cryptographic tokens, dramatically increasing its security as a result. No more than a week later, a concentrated boost of interest from the Asian markets kept the upward trend in motion. From there, a company based in Tokyo announced that plans were in place to create a consortium that would better explore the many ways in which Ripple can be used to create the world's first cryptocurrency debit card.

Ripple is unlike the other cryptocurrencies on this list for several reasons because it operates as a sort of payment network for financial institutions that makes it easier for them to settle transactions between disparate parties than it previously was to a significant degree. Ripple is currently comprised of three different branches. Ripple Labs is the parent company and is where new innovations come from. RippleNet is the payment network for the company that Ripple (the currency) is transferred through and XRP (also known as Ripple, which can be confusing) is the token that is being transferred in the transactions.

The Ripple blockchain operates in much the same way as any other blockchain, except that XRP was not created to serve as a transactional currency. Rather, it was designed as a utility to make it easier for financial institutions to conduct a wide variety of transactions without having to worry about exchanging currencies beforehand. This means that XRP can be thought of as more a type of settlement token than a representation of a currency in its own right.

Because it is not processing transactions in a traditional way, its transactions are mined differently as well. Specifically, no new tokens are generated through the mining process as transactions are instead verified by multiple parties to guarantee that a consensus is maintained. At the time its blockchain came online, there were 100 billion Ripple created, with 60 percent of those remaining in the hands of Ripple Labs. These 60 billion are not considered part of the Ripple Market Cap and are used purely for settlement purposes.

As the speculative market that surrounds XRP in no way affects the success of Ripple Labs, trading in Ripple can be thought of as more analogous to trading in the forex market than other types of cryptocurrencies. New banks are being drawn to Ripple every day because it gives them the ability to move around much more quickly than is otherwise the case because the average Ripple transaction clears in less than five seconds.

Litecoin:

Litecoin is a type of P2P cryptocurrency that allows for low-cost, virtually instantaneous payments between accounts located anywhere in the world. If this is already starting to sound like the pitch for Bitcoin, there is certainly a reason for it. Specifically, Litecoin was originally developed to be the silver to Bitcoin's gold. Over time, however, as Bitcoins structural issues came to light, the relationship between the two has cooled and now many view Litecoin as one of Bitcoin's main competitors.

One of the most important facts about the opensource nature

of the Bitcoin and blockchain code is the fact that anyone can

fork the blockchain and add any new functionality to the

technology that they wish. As such, the Litecoin

cryptocurrency was first released to the public in October of

2011 and is the creation of engineer Charlie Lee, who decided

to decrease the generation time of blocks, increase the total

number of coins and change the verification method to

scrypt in hopes of making it easier for people to mine with

existing hardware. Lee wanted to change the way the

blockchain worked that would be, in his opinion for the

better. Specifically, he was already worried about the amount of time that a new transaction was taking to be verified and wanted to decrease it as much as possible.

Not much speculative interest was shown in Litecoin until November 2013 which the price doubled in less than 24 hours. It reached a $1 billion market cap that same month. Since then, the market cap of Litecoin has more than doubled, leaving it around $2.5 billion by the end of 2017.

The most important innovation that Litecoin brings to the table, and what makes it most worth your consideration, is that it is the first of the highest market cap cryptocurrencies to implement the Segregated Witness (Segwit) technology. This technology is designed to minimize the effect of current size limit caps to the blocks in the blockchain, helping to improve transaction times in the process. This is done by segmenting the transaction between the transaction data and the data required to verify it. This verification data is then returned to the end of the block, causing the blockchain to view it as a different structure. The primary section is then counted as normal, with the verification data only taking up 25 percent of the space than it otherwise would.

Also in Litecoin's favor is what is known as the lightning network which helps to improve transaction speeds across the board. While not yet ready for prime time, when it is rolled out fully it will create a sidechain that smaller and easier to complete transactions will be shunted off to, allowing them to be processed more quickly, while also leaving more primary power available for larger transactions on the primary chain, improving their speed as well.

Finally, when considering the future value of a specific cryptocurrency, it is important to keep in mind that, unlike the Nakamoto alias, Lee is still very much engaged in improving the Litecoin blockchain. This also makes him the most active public face for the Bitcoin blockchain as a whole, simply because no one else has stepped up to fill this role. Having a face for the public to put with the technology could easily prove to be a deciding factor when it comes to adoption on a mass scale.

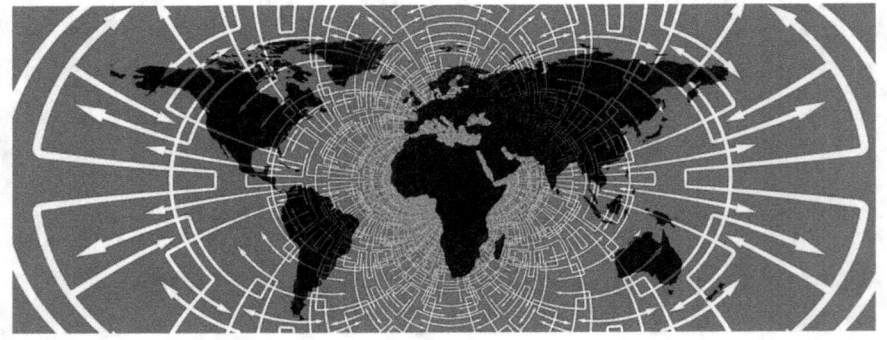

Currently, Lee is working to make the Segwit protocol more popular as it has taken a while to gain mainstream acceptance by Litecoin users. As this is crucial to the successful rollout of the Lightning network, mass adoption is currently at the top of his list of priorities moving forward. The upgrade will go live across the chain as a whole as soon as 75 percent of users signal that they support the chain.

Chapter 3: Investing in Cryptocurrency

Investing in cryptocurrency can be confusing at first because, while it might appear similar to buying stocks from afar, the process is actually quite different. When you buy into a cryptocurrency, rather than buying shares you are buying digital tokens from a third party in exchange for either a fiat currency or your own digital tokens. To further complicate matters, various types of cryptocurrencies have differing transactional purposes, and even those that don't operate as a currency in the traditional sense are still invested in for purely speculative purposes.

What's more, while the amount of conversation around the topic of cryptocurrency makes it seem as though everyone is buying into one type or another, the reality is that only a very small portion of the population is currently using them in any meaningful way. What this means for you is that you still have the opportunity to get in on the ground floor of cryptocurrency as a whole. Sure, there are those out there that have already topped $1,000 or, even, $10,000 per unit, but these are the exception, not the rule.

When this usage rate is compared to their market cap, and the amount of buzz currently surrounding them, it paints a future for cryptocurrency as a whole that is exceedingly bright. As such, while the overall level of volatility for cryptocurrency as a whole remains high, the projected volatility for the future is much lower. That is, of course, until the point of mass saturation hits. When more people are using cryptocurrency than are not, then the pricing bubble that has infused the market since its inception will burst for the last time.

When this occurs, it is highly likely that a vast majority of the cryptocurrencies on the market today will fold in something akin to what occurred during the dotcom crash of the late 1990s. This is why it is important to choose a cryptocurrency that has a demonstrable value as it is far more likely to make it through the coming collapse than one that is based on nothing greater than speculative value.

Choose a cryptocurrency and an exchange: Before you can do anything else, you will want to decide which cryptocurrency will make sense for you, and to do that you will want to first consider just what each cryptocurrency brings to the table. Ideally, you will want to choose something in the price range of your investment capital that will give you the most bang for your buck. If you only have

$1,000 to invest, for example, but nevertheless want to strike while the iron's hot, then buying one ether is likely not the best use of your money. Instead, it would make more sense to start off with around 500 units of Ripple or 1,500 units of Lumens, a smaller cryptocurrency aimed at third world countries that jumped from $0.02 to $.62 per unit between October and December of 2017.

In the previous example, ether, Ripple, and Lumens all have a clear and compelling real-world usage case that gives them value outside of what speculators currently believe they are worth. Ether is used to fuel smart contract transactions and applications running on the Ethereum platform. Ripple is used to facilitate transactions between businesses and Lumens are targeted specifically at a facet of the market that has, up until this point, limited access to traditional banking services that most of the world takes for granted. Choosing a cryptocurrency that has a well-defined reason for being available is crucial to your long-term investing success. Remember, the more useful, the better.

With a cryptocurrency or two in mind, the next thing you will want to do is to consider the various exchanges that offer the cryptocurrency you are interested in. Your options will vary dramatically based on your choice, but if you have a choice, it is important that you do your research and ensure that the exchange is on the level and offers reasonable fees. If you plan on making numerous, smaller transactions, then you will want to find an exchange that offers transactions rates based on a percentage of what the total of the transaction is. If you will be making fewer, larger transactions, then you will want to find an exchange that offers flat rates.

After you have chosen an exchange, you will then need to verify your account, which will often take a few days and require various levels of personal information to ensure you can gain full access to your account. However, if you already have some type of cryptocurrency in hand, you can often start using a new exchange with virtually no verification required.

Once you have gotten your feet wet with a single cryptocurrency, it is also a good idea to diversify, regardless of how much of a good thing your initial investment might seem like up front. Instead, it is almost always going to be more practical to split your total investment capital into at least two places instead of doubling down on what could end up being too much of a "good" thing. This is when creating a portfolio will come into play, and it is a crucial part of investing in the long-term that everyone should consider if they hope to get serious about investing.

Diversifying will also make it easier to protect the profits that you do make from your investments, which should be of utmost concern due to the high level of volatility that all cryptocurrencies have to deal with on a regular basis. The way you should ultimately decide to distribute your money will be a result of your tolerance for risk, how comfortable you are with investing in general and how much time you are willing to commit to micromanaging your investments.

When investing in cryptocurrency, it is also important to take a look at the historical pricing data that is available to ensure that you have a general idea of the type of patterns it moves in on a regular basis. Every cryptocurrency have its own internal flow, and understanding what it is like for the one you choose is key to making the right decisions when the price drops suddenly. If you plan on investing in the long-term, then this type of dip can be expected from time to time, and is, by and large, going to be nothing to worry about. From time to time, however, it could merely represent the tip of a much more precipitous drop, which is what you need to be prepared to identify because no investment remains the right choice forever.

ICOs

Another method of investing in cryptocurrency that is becoming increasingly popular these days is what is known as the initial coin offering, or ICO. In fact, 2017 saw more than a billion dollars raised in this fashion, with notable standouts Bancor and Status.im bringing in $150 million and $75 million in their first 24 hours on the market respectively.

Despite the fact that the name is a play on the concept of the initial public offering, initial coin offerings have little in common with their namesakes save for the name. ICOs are essentially little more than a new way for cryptocurrency and blockchain companies to crowdfund their new ideas. This is done by releasing an early round of the cryptocurrency that will (in theory) be at the heart of this new endeavor at a rate that is (theoretically) going to be far less than what it will be worth when things are up and running.

In exchange for the chance at easy profits, if things go as planned, investors get in on the ground floor, and the company in question gets the money that they need to follow through on the creation of their product or service in the first place. While it is inherently riskier than investing in other types of established cryptocurrencies, it really only requires the cryptocurrency in question to experience one really strong upswing for it to prove profitable in the end. This is far from guaranteed, however. So far, a majority of the movement in the ICO space has been based on the Ethereum platform.

While much of the early ICO funding has come from China, who has long proven to be heavily committed to the advancement of blockchain and cryptocurrency technology, investors from all over the world have been known to open their wallets if the price is right. Nevertheless, before you follow suit, it is important to keep in mind that investing in an ICO naturally comes with a number of different caveats as well.

The first of these is that there have already been inquiries made into several ICOs by the Securities and Exchange Commission regarding an avoidance of regulations including approval of company fundamentals and a business plan that holds water. While they are not held to the same standards as an IPO, what little regulation there is in this sector is already being skirted. Additionally, many analysts note that the initial surge in this arena is likely just another expression of the type of pricing bubble that has plagued cryptocurrency since its inception.

Regardless, this does not mean that the right ICO doesn't have investment potential, as ICOs certainly have the potential to generate significant returns for those who able to look past their additional risk. When it comes to that risk, it is important to keep in mind that the average cryptocurrency is about five times more volatile than gold and nearly 10 times as volatile as the average stock on the S&P 500. This means that when investing in any of the less popular cryptocurrencies you are already stepping well beyond the risk level of what any institutional investor would ever consider. It is important to understand just what you are getting into with an ICO and be fully committed to the idea if you hope to find success in the long-term.

To help ensure you are making the most financially prudent decision possible, approach each and every ICO with an analytical eye. This means you will want to start by taking a closer look at all of the information that is available to you regarding the company in question.

This means you will want to ensure that the business plan with which you are provided is able to show a proven demand for the product or service that the company will be offering and that the numbers make sense in the long-term. It is also very important to ensure that it is easy to see how the cryptocurrency in question fits into the big picture for the company as a whole rather than being tacked on after the fact.

Furthermore, it is important to keep in mind that buying into an ICO in no way provides you any of the benefits commonly associated with an IPO. As such, you won't gain any shares of the company, which also means you will have no say in what the company does moving forward. Without something tangible like stock, you also lose out on the regulations and obligations under which IPOs operate including fiduciary and accreditation requirements. All you get is a smoking deal on a new cryptocurrency, which means it needs to be an extremely good deal for you to take that level of additional risk.

Furthermore, when dealing with an ICO, you can expect to have access to the final product or even a prototype in many instances. In fact, you can consider your ICO, particularly on the ball if you can get a whitepaper, website and business plan out of them all at once. Because you frequently won't have much to go on, it is more important than ever to never invest more in this type of project than you can afford to lose.

Additionally, it is important to not let any of the hype surrounding the company at the time of the ICO influence your decision. After all, there is no guarantee that this level of goodwill and consumer awareness will carry on to the actual release of the product into the wild, especially if that release is years away. All told, it is likely a better choice to put your money elsewhere for the moment, at least until the first round of ICOs comes to market and it becomes clear if any of these early investments will pay off in a meaningful way.

Chapter 4: Trading Cryptocurrency

Scalping

When it comes to trading cryptocurrency effectively, the level of volatility that surrounds the smaller altcoins, 15 percent per day in some cases, means that you need to be ready to move when profits present themselves if you hope to lock them in on a regular basis. If you can regularly manage to be on the ball, however, there is certainly be money to be made from a scalping strategy. In fact, scalping can be effective 24/7 as the cryptocurrency market is always working, and can be effective for both positive and negative trends.

Additionally, due to the small timeframes, you will typically be working with, you will actually find market sentiment more trustworthy which means it actually helps to mitigate a small amount of that pesky volatility when compared to longer holding patterns. It is also an ideal strategy to pursue when you are looking to diversify as it is easy to move between several different markets in a single day.

This type of strategy is not going to be for everyone, however, as it requires a fair amount of active participation as well as plenty of focus and discipline to pull it off successfully. Additionally, scalping requires spending plenty of time on both sides of the emotional spectrum. It comes with a significant rush when the game is afoot, and there is money to be made on the line. On the contrary, however, it will also come with long stretches of boredom where there is nothing to do but stare at numbers on a screen and silently will them to move in the right direction. Overall, a scalping strategy can be successful, but only if you are willing to put in the time to ensure things work out in your favor. You can expect to put in an average of 10 hours per day to make this strategy successful.

Furthermore, if you hope to be successful when it comes to scalping cryptocurrency, you will need to be confident in your ability to set a trading plan from the start and stick to it no matter what. When the numbers align, and it is time to make a move, you won't have time to be thinking through the specifics, and if you don't act, you will miss out. This goes double for exit points as the amount of wiggle room you will have in this situation will be exceedingly slim. If you want to ensure that you don't end up missing out then you will need to give up on the idea of setting a trade and forgetting it, scalping is as active as it gets.

As a general rule, scalping is typically about the quantity of trades over the individual quality of each. Think 10,000 units of cryptocurrency that experience a five percent price increase as opposed to 1,000 units experiencing a 50 percent increase. As such, it is a trading strategy that requires either a larger amount of trading capital to start or a focus on lower-value cryptocurrencies overall where you can more easily deal in the larger trade sizes that scalping requires.

While not a hard and fast rule, scalping strategies typically focus on shorter timeframes, specifically the one and three-minute charts, while using the five and 15-minute charts to follow up and confirm any promising leads. Technical analysis is also going to be the order of the day. That is because nothing in the fundamental analysis will work quickly enough to be useful.

Bollinger bands:

The Bollinger bands will the most useful technical indicator to go along with the scalping strategy. It involves using two standard deviations outside of the simple moving average. Because standard deviation is naturally a measure of volatility the more volatile the market is at the moment, the wider the bands will be and the narrower they are, the less volatile the market is at the moment. Furthermore, the closer the price in question is to the higher of the two bands, the more likely it is that the cryptocurrency is in danger of being overbought. Meanwhile, if the price is closer to the lower of the two bands, then it is likely in danger of being oversold.

The squeeze is the movement at the center of the Bollinger band's success. When the bands come together, they constrict the moving average which, in turn, signals that a period of low volatility is about to conclude, and that increased volatility is on its way, along with all the possibilities that it entails. On the other hand, the wider apart the bands are, the more likely the change is that they decrease in volatility overall, which means it is likely a good time to exit a trade. Nevertheless, this is not a traditional trading signal all by itself, as the bands will give no true indication as to when the change is likely to take place or the direction the price will move in when it does move.

Using Bollinger bands for a scalping strategy:

To make use of Bollinger bands in your scalping strategy, you need to focus on a pair of Bollinger bands that encompass an exponential moving average. This strategy will work with virtually all timeframes and with any cryptocurrency, though it tends to be most effective in the five-minute and three-minute timeframes. To begin this strategy, you will want to use a traditional Bollinger band setup including a default 20 periods along with a standard deviation of two for the first band and 21 periods with a standard deviation of three for second band.

The goal here should be pinpoint periods where the price sits between the pair of standard deviations. After you have found one of these moments you will then want to use a moving average of 200 to monitor the trends changes. If the price rises from the targeted point, you will be able to turn a profit from long position and if it drops you will profit from short positions. Additionally, you will want to keep in mind that if the candle forms inside the existing deviation then the trend is likely to continue while if it forms outside, then it is almost always going to reverse instead.

When these conditions are met, you can rest assured that entering a trade when the next candle forms is a safe choice as it will only open you up to a small amount of additional risk. You will, however, still want to place a stop loss based on the apparent strength of the trend you are keeping an eye on. You will also want to set a target at the point that marks the average of the Bollinger bands, with a second target at the line of the Bollinger band the trend is more likely to intersect with. This strategy is known to be extremely effective, as long as you take into account the price only as it relates to the moving average of 200. As it can be complicated to get a handle on, at first, it is suggested that you practice with this strategy using a number of smaller trades until you are comfortable with the process.

Longer strategy:

While not quite as short as the traditional scalping strategy, the one-hour strategy works off a strict 50 pips goal for each trade, so its overall effectiveness balances out. As the timeframe is naturally longer, it is recommended that you only use it with cryptocurrencies that are experiencing a lull in volatility. Whether buying or selling, if the current trend is bullish and the price is touching the band, you will want to generate an order using a stop loss that is 35 pips lower (or higher depending on the trend).

From there, you will then want to set an exit point that is 50 pips further along in the direction of the trend to guarantee that you cash out when you hit your profit goal. This doesn't mean you can set it and forget it, however, as you will also want to be on hand to sell if the trend reverses or if the price reaches the other band as this could indicate that the trend will end with a breakout in the opposite direction of the trend you were following, the ultimate losing proposition.

Extreme scalping:

To use this strategy successfully, you will want to start by setting both of your Bollinger bands to 21 periods with a two standard deviation. This strategy typically proves to be the most effective in the one-minute timeframe. With this strategy you will want to wait for the price to move within range of one of the Bollinger band at the same time the RSI either increase above 70 for a positive trend, or below 30 for a negative trend. The best-case scenario for this type of strategy is a price point that is in the dead center of the pair of bands with stop losses set five pips above and five pips below the target.

Arbitrage

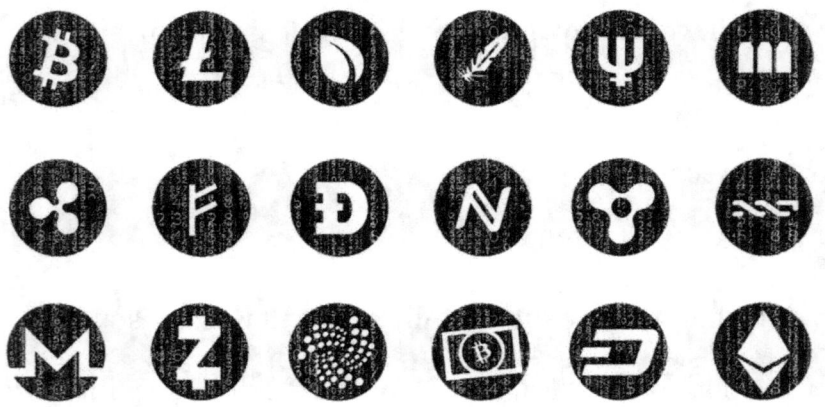

There are more than 100 different cryptocurrency exchanges operating online as of January 2018, and, by and large, it is a miracle if the prices of the major cryptocurrencies line up with one another, much less the smaller ones. What's more, the number of factors in play, the type of traders on each exchange, the rate of various associated cryptocurrencies, even the time of day in the exchange's primary market, all come together to mean that these types of differences happen dozens of times, if not more every day and they stick around long enough to allow eagle-eyed traders to take advantage of them.

For example, the day Bitcoin reached $10,000 on a South Korean Exchange, it spent more than an hour trading at about $250 less than that across many US exchanges. If the market can't naturally work to close a disparity of this magnitude on the most watched cryptocurrency in the world, it doesn't take much of a leap to consider what the smaller cryptocurrencies are up to.

While this is all well and good, perhaps the best news to those considering this type of approach is that the average trader is not overly accustomed to arbitrage and the institutional traders have not yet jumped on the cryptocurrency bandwagon. As such, the market is currently wide open to this type of trading strategy, likely as open as it is ever going to get. Goldman Sachs and other major trading firms are targeting 2018 dates for their own cryptocurrency desks which means it isn't a question of if institutional traders will invest in cryptocurrency, but when the profits are simply too much to resist.

When it comes to cryptocurrency trading, one particularly useful type of arbitrage is what is known as statistical arbitrage which involves looking for opportunities for profit that naturally arise from exchange rate discrepancies as indicated by predicted or historical norms. Unlike other types of arbitrage, statistical arbitrage does involve a small amount of risk because the spreads it concerns itself with could potentially narrow instead of widening. Regardless, the overall profits from this type of arbitrage tend to remain higher, so the average amount of risk works out to be about the same.

To get started using statistical arbitrage, you will want to take a look at historical statistics as well as relevant mathematical modeling techniques, paying special attention to the spread between the various cryptocurrency spreads to determine point where they appear out of line. With the understanding that these disparities are likely going to narrow over time, there are several ways of taking advantage of this fact, the first of which is called market neutral arbitrage.

Market neutral arbitrage involves taking a long position on a cryptocurrency that is currently undervalued based on historical precedent, while at the same shorting a second cryptocurrency that appears, historically, to be over-valued. The cryptocurrencies you choose should have similar properties so that an increase in one causes a decrease in the other.

Cross-market arbitrage is a fancy name for keeping track of market prices across various exchanges before buying near the historic low in one exchange and selling during a historic high on another. The lows and highs don't need to be this extreme to see real results; any steady price difference can be worthwhile, especially if you are in a position to capitalize on it in a serious way.

Pairs trading statistical arbitrage is a more advanced version of the strategy which places assets into appropriate pairs based on their fundamental similarities. When a specific half of a cryptocurrency pair outperforms the other, the weaker of the two will then be bought based on the assumption that it will move in the opposite direction of the over-performing partner. This position is then hedged because any market changes can be countered by shorting the cryptocurrency that is over-performing. Because of a large number of cryptocurrencies that can be involved in a statistical arbitrage strategy, the high portfolio turnover and the fairly small size of the spread one is trying to capture, the strategy is often implemented in an automated fashion, and great attention is placed on reducing trading costs.

Conclusion

Thank you for making it through to the end of *Cryptocurrency: Best Strategies for Investing and Profiting from Cryptocurrency*, let's hope it was informative and able to provide you with all of the tools you need to achieve your goals, whatever it is that they may be. Just because you've finished this book doesn't mean there is nothing left to learn on the topic, expanding your horizons is the only way to find the mastery you seek.

When investing in more traditional assets, it is perfectly feasible to reach a general level of familiarity with a number of strategies that work for you and never learn anything else while still finding success. Investing in the cryptocurrency market does not work this way, unfortunately, simply because so much about the market is new and prone to change without notice. As such, if you hope to find success when it comes to investing in cryptocurrency it is important you commit yourself to learning as much about the topic as possible, and stick with it.

Whether you invest in cryptocurrency or not, that is all up to you. Remember, though, that while cryptocurrency *could* make you money, it *may* also lose you big time. Don't be discouraged! You could avoid losing money in cryptocurrency as long as you use it the right way.

The next best thing to do now is to get started making money from cryptocurrency in the way that makes the most sense to you. When doing so, it is important to approach the entire affair with the right mindset and goals based on the amount of time you plan on investing for. While some cryptocurrencies are always going to be prone to sudden, significant, swings in price, they are undoubtedly the exception, not the rule. If you go into cryptocurrency investment with the assumption that you will become a millionaire overnight, not only are you going to be disappointed, but you will be far more likely to make mistakes based on approach centered around this assumption. Instead, it is far better to think of investing in cryptocurrency as a marathon, not a sprint, slow and steady wins the race.

The future of cryptocurrency remains unknown. But we can be confident that these digital currencies could make a great impact in our economy and finance system.

Finally, if you found this book useful in any way, a review on Amazon is always appreciated!